WALKABOUT

Weather

Editor: **Ambreen Husain**
Design: **Volume One**

Photographs: Bruce Coleman Ltd.—(J. Fry) 5,
(G. Ahrens) 19, (C. James) 22; Eye Ubiquitous—
(D. Fobister) 30; Chris Fairclough Colour Library—
5 inset, 10; Robert Harding—9, (G. White) 20, 27,
28; Hutchison Library—(B. Regent) 14 inset; Frank
Lane Picture Agency—(M. Nimmo) 11, (D. Jones)
15, (G. Nystrand) 17, (E. & D. Hosking) 26;
Oxford Scientific Films—(E. Robinson) 8; Photri
Inc.—(Skjold) 31; Science Photo Library—(C. & M.
Perennou) 14; Swift Picture Library—(M. Read) 6,
7, (G. Dore) 21; ZEFA—4, 12-13, 16, 18, 23, 24,
25, 29.

Library of Congress Cataloging-in-Publication Data

Pluckrose, Henry Arthur.
    Weather / by Henry Pluckrose.
      p.   cm. — (Walkabout)
    ISBN 0-516-08123-3
    1. Weather—Juvenile literature.
  2. Meteorology—Juvenile literature. [1. Weather.
  2. Meteorology.] I. Title. II. Series: Pluckrose,
Henry Arthur. Walkabout.
  QC981.3.P57   1994
  551.5—dc20   93-45660
                                                CIP
                                                AC

1994 Childrens Press® Edition
© 1993 Watts Books, London
All rights reserved. Printed in the United States of America.
Published simultaneously in Canada.
    2 3 4 5 6 7 8 9 0 R 03 02 01 00 99 98 97 96 95

WALKABOUT Weather

Henry Pluckrose

CHILDRENS PRESS®
CHICAGO

Have you ever thought
how different the
weather can be?
In summertime
the days are warm.

In wintertime the days
are often cold.
We use a thermometer
to find out how hot or
how cold it is.
A thermometer
measures temperature.

If the weather is very dry and very hot, the sun dries up rivers and ponds.
The soil cracks.
Plants cannot grow without water.

Sometimes, if there is too much rain, rivers overflow their banks. Floods can cause a lot of damage.

7

In very cold weather,
water freezes.
Ponds and rivers are
covered with a thin
layer of ice.
Animals and birds die if
they cannot find food.
The most pleasant days
are not too hot and not
too cold.

What sort of
weather is this?
Very wet!

Clouds like these
bring rain.
When dark clouds form
there may be a storm.

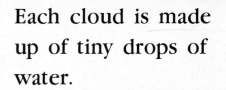

Each cloud is made up of tiny drops of water.
These drops of water join up and become bigger and heavier.
Heavy drops of water fall to the ground . . . as rain.

11

Roofs, roads, and fields
do not stay wet . . .
even after a hard rain.
The sun warms the
water in puddles,
ponds, rivers, lakes,
and seas.
The water changes into
water vapor.
This damp air rises.
As it cools it turns into
tiny drops of water
that form clouds.

If it is very cold, the water in the clouds turns to ice.
The ice crystals join and form six-pointed snowflakes.
These snowflakes fall from the clouds.
If they stay cold they fall as snow.

Sometimes the rain freezes
as it falls. This is hail.
Hailstones are balls of ice.

When it is very cold,
frost forms on the
ground and on plants . . .

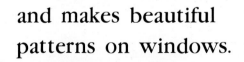

and makes beautiful
patterns on windows.

If you look up at clouds,
you will see that they
are moving.
Winds blow clouds
across the sky.
Wind is moving air.

You cannot see the
wind, but you can see
leaves and grasses
shiver as the wind
moves through them.

19

Scientists who study the
weather use a special
machine that measures
the speed of the wind.
It is called an anemometer.
If the wind is blowing hard,
the cups spin very quickly.

20

The weather vane also
tells us something
about the wind.
It shows the direction from
which the wind is blowing.

When the wind is blowing
hard, we say that the weather
is stormy.
Strong winds can uproot trees
and even lift roofs off houses.

Some storms are noisy.
Electricity builds up in
storm clouds as they
move together.
The electricity must find
its way to earth.
We see it flash
as lightning.
We hear it as thunder.

Sometimes there is no wind.
The air feels cool and damp.
When the weather is misty
we cannot see very far.
Drivers must be extra
careful.

In towns and cities, smoke and fumes from factories and cars can become trapped close to the ground. This dirty air is called smog.

Scientists who study the
weather are called
meteorologists.
They collect information
from weather stations . . .

and from satellites flying
high above the ground.
They use all the information
they collect to prepare
a weather forecast.

The weather forecast
helps farmers decide
what work can be done
in the fields . . .

and helps fishermen decide whether to go out to sea.

The weather affects what we
wear and what we do.
Weather is important
to all living things.

But we cannot control the weather. What kind of weather do you like best?

Index

About this book

Young children acquire information in a casual, almost random fashion. Indeed, they learn just by being alive! The books in this series complement the way young children learn. Through photographs and a simple text the readers are encouraged to comment on the world around them.

To a young child, the world is new and almost everything in it is interesting. But interest alone is not enough. If a child is to grow intellectually this interest has to be directed and extended. This book uses a well-tried and successful method of achieving this goal. By focusing on a particular topic, it invites the reader first to look and then to question. The words and photographs provide a starting point for discussion.

Children enjoy information books just as much as stories and poetry. For those who are not yet able to read print, this book provides pictures that encourage talk and visual discrimination—a vital part of the learning process.

Henry Pluckrose